Peaceful Communication In Marriage

Gently Rebuilding Trust and Intimacy in Relationships

Vishal Pandey

Copyright © 2019 by Vishal Pandey. All Rights Reserved.

No reproduction without permission.

No part of this book may be reproduced, transmitted, downloaded, decompiled, reversed engineered, or stored in or introduced into any information storage & retrieval system, in any form or by any means, without expressed written permission of the author.

The scanning, uploading and distribution of this book via internet or any other means, without the permission of the author is illegal and punishable by law. Please purchase only authorized editions and do not participate in, or encourage, piracy of copyrighted materials.

Disclaimer: Author does not assume any responsibility for any errors or omissions, nor does he represent or warrant that the information, ideas, plans, actions, suggestions and methods of operations contained herein is in all cases true, accurate, appropriate or legal. It is the reader's responsibility to consult with his or her advisors before applying any of the information contained in this book. The information included in this book is not intended to serve as a legal advice and author disclaims any liability resulting from the use or application of the contained information.

Email: yourselfactualization@gmail.com

TABLE OF CONTENTS

Introduction

PART 1: Understanding Your Partner and Yourself

Chapter 1 - Acknowledging And Accepting Your Partner

Chapter 2 - Love Is Never About Taking

Chapter 3 - Become More Self-Aware

Chapter 4 - The Secret To Love

Chapter 5 - To Give Love To Others, You Must Love Yourself

Chapter 6 - Your Life Situation Plays A Critical Role

Chapter 7 - Being Attracted To Other People Is Fine

PART 2: Pitfalls to Avoid

Chapter 8 - If Any Topic Comes Up Repeatedly, Take It Seriously

Chapter 9 - Let Sleeping Dogs Lie

Chapter 10 - The Role Of Bad Habits

Chapter 11 - How Money Problems Affect Your Relationship?

Chapter 12 - Impact Of Health Problems On Your Relationship

Chapter 13 - Never Take Relationships For Granted

Chapter 14 - Dealing With A Broken Heart

Chapter 15- The War For Control

Chapter 16 - The Fear Of Losing Your Partner

Chapter 17 - Small Mistakes That Can Harm A Relationship

PART 3: Creating a Fulfilling Relationship

Chapter 18 - Be Open With Your Partner

Chapter 19 - Express Your Love

Chapter 20 - Importance Of Special Time Together

Chapter 21 - The Importance Of Eye Contact

Chapter 22 - Touch Builds Intimacy

Chapter 23 - Listen Intently

Chapter 24 - Regular Statements Of Affection

Chapter 25 - The Significance Of Time And Date

Chapter 26 - Keeping Your Commitments

Chapter 27 - Do Things For Each Other

Chapter 28 - Surprise Each Other

Chapter 29 - Encourage And Compliment

Chapter 30 - Role Of Personal Growth

Conclusion

More Books by the Author

INTRODUCTION

"Why do we have arguments, disputes & differences when we love each other?"

"Why do I not feel loved anymore?"

"Why do we keep fighting all the time? We never used to fight in the beginning. What has changed?"

These are some critical questions we face while being in a long term relationship. Everyone is confused. Everyone is asking around. We ask our friends for their advice. We go see counselors. We seek advice online.

There are several studies conducted on maintaining a healthy relationship. There are many talk shows, books and online articles on the subject, then why are people still looking for a solution? Even after receiving all these tips and techniques, why do we feel like we are still missing something?

The answer to all of these questions is that the majority of the advice we receive, tends to revolve around changing our external behavior.

"Be honest."

"Support each other."

"Give each other some space."

"Say sorry."

While seemingly good advice, these changes do not stick for long because nothing has changed internally. We are still the same person inside. We still have our old mindset, perception, beliefs, and values.

As long as we don't get to the root of the problem, no amount of tips & tricks will work long term. We have to go beneath the surface and find the underlying cause of problems in our relationships.

And that is the subject of this book.

Because the will to have a healthy, loving relationship is one of the primary desires of every human being, most of us are willing to do everything in our power to improve our relationships. We just need someone to point us in the right direction.

You both have underlying needs

Both you & your partner have specific needs & desires in a relationship. After struggling with relationships for a long time, I stumbled upon the fact that ultimately, all relationship issues can be traced back to the needs of the partners not being met.

"Love is never about taking. It's always about giving."

This book is all about understanding yourself and your partner so the differences between you two can be sorted out from the very roots.

Here are a few things we'll be going through:

- What does your partner need from you? What do they want out of the relationship to feel happy & content?

- How to find what your partner needs and what can you do to fulfill those needs?

- How to peacefully sort out the situation when you & your partner get in an argument?

- How to have a balanced relationship where both partners are equal and feel content?

- How do external factors like financial problems, bad habits, and health issues affect the happiness of your relationships?

- If you have been hurt in a past relationship, you'll stop yourself from fully opening up to your current partner. Learn how to let go of the past and open your heart to give and receive love.

- You and your partner WILL have differences. How to become okay with that and still love them?

- Why you must love yourself to be able to love the other person? You cannot pour water into someone else's cup if your own is empty.

- How to never take a relationship for granted, no matter how old it is? The more committed you are, the more blissful your relationship would be.

Love in a relationship is different from anything else, and you can't treat it like something you might have "accomplished" before. Love is pure, it is accepting, it is forgiving, and it is open to the lover's **thoughts** and **needs** at all times. Anything else is not love but only a distortion. Anything not love is simply a relationship of another sort, i.e., a living arrangement, roommate agreement, or work relationship designed to complete a given task, such as raising kids.

If you would like to thrive on finding new ways to love your partner, you need to prepare each aspect of yourself for the rare challenge that building a loving relationship presents.

Since you are reading this book, and are open to building a loving relationship, you want your relationship to be an empowering, positive aspect of your life, not a liability.

Relationships do not get better by chance. They get better by change.

You can't expect to see change if you never do anything differently. Make a firm commitment that you are going to do a few things daily to improve your relationship.

I promise you that it is worth it. Once in a lifetime, you met someone who changed everything in your life. Do not let them drift away without doing your best to make things right.

Are you with me on that one?

Let's begin.

PART 1: Understanding Your Partner and Yourself

CHAPTER 1

Acknowledging And Accepting Your Partner

"It is not our differences that divide us. It is our inability to recognize, accept, and celebrate those differences" ~Audre Lorde

In the beginning, there were similarities...

Early in your relationship, you and your partner probably rejoiced when you discovered shared interests: "I can't believe you like foreign films too--it was such a downer that my last boyfriend said he should not have to read his movies!"

And when gaping differences happened to peek through (you're a devout meat eater and he's a strict vegetarian), you abandoned your previous convictions with glee ("I can't believe you're a vegetarian. I've been thinking of giving up meat for the last thirteen years but it never seemed like a good time--until now!")

Love propels you to create similarities where none exist.

Intimacy - the emotional, physical and, for some, spiritual connection couples share - is effortless when relationships are new. You feel like you can talk for hours, you experience intense passion, and you want to spend all your free time together.

And as the relationship progresses, you may find yourself minimizing the fact that your once-communicative partner now prefers television to talking or that the frequency of lovemaking continues to decline.

And then there were differences...

If you and your partner have been in the relationship for more than two years, you've come to realize that there are differences between the two of you. Since you're human beings (and, like snowflakes, no two are alike), there's no way around that fact. However, you can be different and still be compatible.

Hopefully, you and your partner are compatible in the areas that matter to you both - core values and life goals.

The good news is that certain differences can actually be beneficial. For instance, what's difficult for you might come easy to your partner--her/his personality complements yours: she's talkative/you're quiet; you're playful/he's serious; she's a saver/you're a spender; you're shy/he's outgoing; you're nervous/she's calm.

Unfortunately, differences can also fan the flames of conflict. For instance, the quietness you once described as "charming" can someday frustrate you to no end--especially when it takes all your emotional energy just to get your partner to have a conversation.

The Importance of Accepting Differences

Couples often enter counseling with a long wish-list detailing why and how the other person should change. These may seem like reasonable requests, but often real change doesn't happen because the couple is attempting to close the gap on the inherent differences that define each person - differences that were not obvious or that they overlooked early in the relationship. Such futile efforts (trying to change the unchangeable) merely work to build resentments and break apart intimacy.

A alternative solution is to work toward accepting the differences that exist. The art of acceptance is essential for a healthy relationship. Acceptance should be an essential part of your relationship toolbox, along with your (and your partner's) willingness to compromise and negotiate.

The payoff to the road of acceptance is a stronger, more fulfilling relationship.

5 ways to be more accepting to your partner

1. The most important step is to cultivate a mindset of openness. You cannot move forward unless you make a daily, conscious effort to open your heart to all of your partner - even the parts of him/her that you wish didn't exist.

2. There are as many pathways to intimacy as there are people walking the earth. Differences between how you and your partner achieve intimacy are just that, differences. They do not imply right versus wrong--so suspend your judgement.

3. Acceptance is not submissive complacency. In essence, you are allowing yourself to co-exist peacefully with all that you cannot control in your relationship.

4. Working toward acceptance doesn't mean you have to blindly accept everything about your partner that you find troubling and never challenge your partner to improve. Relationships are about compromise and change. If there is something your partner can change that would improve the relationship (i.e., quitting smoking), you should encourage that.

5. Acceptance and appreciation go hand-in-hand. When you begin to accept all the different ways in which you and your partner experience and express love, you have taken the vital step toward appreciating your partner's uniqueness.

Developing a mindset of acceptance is a process--with starts and stops. The solution to moving forward is to become mindful each time you fall into a judgmental mindset. With practice, you will embrace the inherent differences that make you and your partner unique.

CHAPTER 2

Love Is Never About Taking

One of the concerning issues with intimate relationships today is that many people look at relationships as... "*what's in it for me?*" Not a helpful mindset at all. We should wake up each day trying to figure out **what we can do to help make our partner's life better**. If we don't, it will eventually cause conflicts which could take the relationship apart. In other words, it can't just be about you - it has to be about both people getting their needs met.

To have a healthy relationship, it must be based on give and take. Each partner should be putting in 100%, rather than the common idea of being a 50/50 compromise. You put in 100% and expect your partner to do the same.

1. The first thing you have to know about give and take is that you need to recognize what is important to your significant other. If you really know them, you know what's important to them and what they need & want in the relationship. If you focus on helping your partner get what they need and want, they will be much more likely to focus on helping you with what you need & want. That's a win for both of you.

2. Another common problem within a relationship is trying to win every argument. Here's the truth about arguments - Even if you win an argument, you'll lose respect in the eyes of your partner.

When you argue with your spouse or significant other, there should be no winner or loser. If you feel like you won an argument, it's likely your significant other feels like they lost. If you are in a truly loving relationship, you would never want your partner to feel sad or upset. It's about understanding their point of view; see where they are coming from. More on that later.

3. Third, you must learn how to effectively resolve conflict. You have to fight your ego when it comes to a relationship, or you risk the other person feeling upset. Don't attack your partner verbally, and certainly not physically. You should be able to see their perspective and respect it. That is part of being in a mature relationship.

It's never wise to drag out old arguments that have already been settled. When you agree to settle an argument, it should be wiped away and never brought up again. Focus on the issue at hand, and continue to respect your partner throughout. Even when you are angry or upset, respect should still be there.

As you can see, healthy relationships only work if there is a give & take by both partners. If you feel like you have to win all the time or take control of the relationship, that points to deeper issues. Why do you feel the need to take control? Why can't we just let our partners be and enjoy their company without any agenda?

Let's go deeper.

CHAPTER 3

Become More Self-Aware

A significant part of couple therapy involves improving self-awareness. Because you cannot fix a problem until you are aware of its source, it is important to understand what drives you so you can better control your subconscious impulses.

For example, people develop survival strategies during interpersonal conflict in an effort to protect oneself from a perceived threat. Common survival strategies include defensiveness, withdrawal, or counterattack. Partners are often unaware of these impulses in the moment and naturally focus on what the other partner is doing to trigger them.

It takes two to overcome a maladaptive conflict sequence, and becoming self-aware of the vulnerabilities being triggered and how you slide into unhealthy survival strategies is the first step in changing the sequence.

Self-awareness is important to relationships, and it is something you are in complete control of. It can feel difficult and overwhelming to try and increase awareness of something that feels so automatic and deeply ingrained. It is not uncommon to experience shame around a particular survival strategy, and it takes courage to share this with your partner.

These exercises would improve your self-awareness in your relationship:

1. Get to know your story:

How well do you know what impacts your automatic way of interacting with your partner? These behaviors often stem from early childhood experiences and previous relationships. Take some time to delve into your personal history and better understand how early events influence your perceptions, expectations, and behavior in your current relationship.

Here are some helpful questions to answer about yourself, adapted from The Seven Principles for Making Marriage Work by John Gottman:

What difficult periods have you gone through? How did you make it through these traumas? What are the lasting effects on you?

What behaviors have you developed to try and protect yourself from future hurt?

How did your family express emotion when you were a child? What is your own philosophy about expressing feelings?

What differences exist between you and your partner in expressing emotion? How do you make sense of these differences?

2. Practice mindfulness:

Mindfulness techniques, which aims to improve openness and awareness in the moment, are helpful in identifying triggers and underlying vulnerabilities. Because mindfulness helps you stay present, improving mindfulness skills will help you in mapping out your role in conflict sequences and point out potential turning points where you can learn to respond in a healthier way.

It also helps slow down reactionary responses so partners can pause the conversation and check interpretations before acting on false assumptions. Increase your self-awareness through mindfulness activities such as meditation or breathing exercises.

If you wish to learn more on meditation and related exercises, check out my book "*Positive Thinking: How To Stop Focusing On Nonsense And Live A Better Life*"

3. Be open and actively seek feedback:

Your partner has a front row seat to the way you interact and can be a helpful tool in increasing self-awareness. Try to establish a safe, open dialogue with your partner to discuss problems with communication and possible solutions.

This requires you to open yourself to potentially negative and hurtful feedback, and you may not always like what you hear. Become aware of any tendencies to justify or defend actions that your partner finds problematic, and work together to see how each of you can alter the conflict sequence.

When offering feedback to your partner, be considerate of how you communicate your opinion. Do not just point out things your partner does wrong, as you are not meant to serve as the judge. It is helpful to highlight things your partner did that were hurtful and to make an effort to better understand what drives such behavior. Come to these discussions with an open mind and the goal to better understand your partner. You will benefit greatly when your partner returns the favor.

CHAPTER 4

The Secret To Love

In our world of fast food, Twitter messages of 140 characters, high-speed Internet connections, everything in our lives is available "on demand", we seek instant gratification in all things. Our relationships are no different, we seek the magic bullet or the simple little pill to swallow to make our troubles go away and transform our relationships.

Is there really a secret to loving well and having a successful relationship? Yes, there is a secret:

It's not about you.

Take a step away from your current relationship and ponder for a moment. Who is being served in your relationship? Are you waiting for your partner to step up and answer to your needs and demands, meanwhile withholding *your* love and affection until they do?

It comes back to the same mindset time and time again. Marriage and relationships are not based on meeting your partner half way, each giving as little as possible to get what they desire in return. Scores are kept and the focus is on meeting personal needs and loving your partner equally in return, sometimes one gesture at a time.

Successful relationships require both partners to give completely of themselves first. It's not about you, it is about serving and honoring each other. Try it for a day or two and watch what happens in your relationship. Without asking for anything from your partner simply do your best to try to anticipate and fulfill their needs. Most likely your partner will begin to reciprocate without even realizing they are doing so.

This is a turning point in many relationships. Over time it becomes easier to serve each other and once on this path it is more comfortable to openly discuss what you are both able and willing to do to please each other.

CHAPTER 5

To Give Love To Others, You Must Love Yourself

We have heard the idea of loving ourselves first in order to love and be loved by another. Yet how many of us are truly engaged in the practice of being loving and kind to ourselves? Being completely loving and kind to ourselves no matter what, being committed to tend to and to express our own needs and desires and show up for ourselves is the foundation required to draw in love and relationship.

Here's what so many of us do:

We beat ourselves up constantly

We tell ourselves the worst stories

We tell ourselves what we should have done differently, how someone else would have done it better, how there must be something wrong with us, how if only we were prettier, fitter, more lovable, a good person or were different to who we are in some way, all would be well.

We criticize ourselves

We compare ourselves to others

We put all of our focus on our flaws and imperfections

We put huge pressure and expectation on ourselves to be perfect

We don't take time to celebrate our accomplishments

We constantly make ourselves wrong

When we are looking to draw in love and relationship into our lives, we are called to start clearly seeing the way in which we are treating ourselves.

I clearly remember when a friend of mine, Priyanka, started to see that everything she thought men were doing to her, for example: abandoning her, rejecting her, not valuing her, not seeing her etc, she was in fact doing to herself.

It was being reflected back to her by men all around her. In her commitment and intention for love, she had to take a radical new stand for herself, that she would absolutely show up for herself, knowing that if she wanted to create the type of relationship and connection that she was yearning for, she would need to become deeply connection to herself.

Enough was enough. She was no longer willing to negate or dismiss her own feelings or needs. She started to become deeply interested and curious about all of the ways in which she was currently doing this. She became deeply engaged in loving, giving, listening to her own needs and desires. She started making new choices and taking new actions that were in alignment with what she was seeing and her commitment to transforming her experience of love. She was taking a radical stand for herself.

When we change the relationship we have with ourselves, our whole external world changes accordingly.

This was truly miraculous. She told me she remembers the first time she discovered this truth. Having been deeply in the process of giving to and nurturing herself, she began to put herself into the dating world again.

Only now one thing was different.

Her.

She had a real sense of her own value and what she wanted to create in a relationship. She was able to express her needs and desires, what she needed in relationship and what she had to bring to a relationship. She became wholly visible.

She noticed that now she was attracting a very different kind of man: men who really saw her, who like her, were genuinely interested in having a relationship. She attracted men who were "lit up" by her, who could not wait to get to know her. Her whole experience of love and relationship was transformed and it wasn't too long before she met the love of her life.

How can we start to change our relationship with ourselves?

It begins with awareness. Start noticing all of the ways in which you dismiss your own needs.

Without blaming or shaming yourself, ask yourself: "In what ways to I beat myself up and criticize myself?"

Take a radical new stand for yourself, your happiness and well being by showing up for yourself no matter what.

Start telling yourself how attractive and valuable you are.

Become available and committed to yourself.

Take the time to celebrate your achievements.

Spend time doing things you love and enjoy.

Have play time.

Learn to say "no".

Set new boundaries and limits where appropriate.

Start to catch yourself when you judge or criticize yourself, take a step back and ask "What advice I would give in this situation to a person who I loved a lot?"

You'll come up with a much more loving response.

CHAPTER 6

Your Life Situation Plays A Critical Role

Right now we are all living in a fast-paced world. The stresses of daily living are demanding and it is easy to put "taking care of self" on the back burner. Life can feel like one is on a constant treadmill being pulled in many directions. The key to success in work and personal relationships is to be centered and calm in spite of the daily concerns.

Regain Control Over Your Life

Here are some ways to regain control over your life.

1. Give Yourself Permission to Make Time for Yourself

Your mindset lays the foundation for how you will care for yourself. If you see yourself mainly as having to meet the deadlines and demands of others you will end up feeling out of control. Give yourself permission to re-center your life. How do you want to live? When do you feel taken advantage of? You alone can decide what is right for you and what you are able to do. Set few minutes a day aside to think about what would help you to get centered and feel in-charge of your life.

2. Structure Simplifies Life

You will find that by organizing your surroundings you will start feeling lighter. Start out by making one little adjustment each day and before long you will feel more in control of your life. Have a regular time for eating and going to bed and getting up. Pay attention to how much time you are spending watching TV which can become a time robber. Use a calendar to keep track of appointments. Schedule your day. See how much time you are spending in different activities and sort them out in a structure that allows for better control over the day.

3. Re-focus on Taking Care of Yourself

Find ways to create energy for yourself. In order to be fully engaged in life you have to be energized. Some ways of creating energy are by eating healthfully, exercising regularly, being intellectually engaged, having friends, and being involved in the community.

In my book 'The H*appiness Edge*', I have extensively covered how to recharge your emotional energy as well as physical to achieve a balanced, healthy life.

4. Cultivate a Positive Attitude

We all have control over our attitude. It is not something that is predetermined by genetics and the environment. You can take control of your attitude. You may have to unlearn some habits which do not serve you well. For instance, if you are used to putting yourself down and measuring yourself against others you may want to rethink that. It is your job to treat yourself as your own best friend.

By refocusing on caring for yourself you will start to feel more in control of your life and the direction it is taking. The key is to do things consistently and before long you will feel lighter and happier and have vibrant relationships.

Stress and how it affects your relationships

Stress plays a big part in ruining our health. The effects of stress on the body are potentially deadly. But it doesn't end there. It also affects our relationships.

The stress you are under has an effect on every person you come in contact with. Especially your closest family and friends, and not in a good way.

Reducing your stress levels is a must if you want to have joy-filled relationships.

Reducing stress will improve your relationships in the following ways:

1. You will be more relaxed and loving. Stress puts you in a bad mood & suppresses your ability to express love & care towards others. This is especially important when you are dealing with family & friends. Your lack of warmth could affect how you treat people.

2. You will be less distracted. The stressful situation is always on your mind, even when you are not directly thinking about it. So when you are trying to enjoy time with family and friends, there's always a part of you that is being distracted by it. And the effect on other people is that you aren't paying attention.

3. You will be more focused. Your close ones want your full attention. When something is always at the back of your mind, you just can't focus on the people who are very important to you. This can lead to more drama, which only increases your stress.

So eliminating the stress in other areas of your life will greatly improve your relationships. One excellent way to eliminate stress is to improve your creative thinking. It will give you more options to cope with stress.

By strengthening your creative thinking, you can see more solutions to your stressful situation. You can see alternate ways of doing things which can lead to reduced stress. And sometimes, just realizing that you have options makes the stress easier to handle.

When approaching stress, you need to answer the question "how am I feeling right now?" If you are generally satisfied with how you feel during your day, you are doing great.

If you are not, you could look at a comprehensive stress management system, that uses creative thinking, time management, meditation, and other components together to eliminate stress.

CHAPTER 7

Being Attracted To Other People Is Fine

Infidelity, cheating, and affairs . . . these are topics that we tiptoe around discussing when we're in relationships. The prospect of being lied to and cheated on by our significant others is not only a terrifying prospect to dwell on, but it's an even more frightening notion to consider committing against those we love. It's no wonder that we are so averse to exploring this topic in our everyday lives!

The truth is that life is capricious and unpredictable, and while many of us are under the illusion that avoiding what makes us feel uncomfortable and embarrassed is the solution, we really need to have an open conversation that explores this taboo—and much feared—area of life.

It's time that we stop ignoring the ominous "elephant in the room," and start exploring why we feel so ashamed about feeling attracted to other people in loving relationships.

If you feel distressed, depraved, guilty or embarrassed for feeling attracted to others in your loving relationship, don't allow your conscience to continue withering under the weight of your shame. Keep reading to discover why it is not only OK to feel attracted to others but why it is normal as well.

Let me share with you something about myself. I am fortunate enough to currently be in a very loving, very satisfying long-term relationship that I never thought was possible to have with another human being. So I was very shocked and very surprised when I began to feel attracted to other people in my life. To my horror I found (and continue to find), that I feel intellectually, emotionally and physically attracted to others in my life completely out of the blue and with no warning whatsoever.

"What the hell is WRONG with me?" I have wondered many times before, "Why do I feel this way? I SHOULDN'T feel this way." And so ensues the endless hours of self-criticism and merciless put-downs.

Does this sound familiar to you?

If you have made feeling attracted to other people a crime in your life, you will most likely feel dirty, flawed, and irredeemably guilty like I have often felt before. Furthermore, you were probably indoctrinated with the unrealistic, fantasy-land ideal of "True love means that it is IMPOSSIBLE for you to be attracted to others."

Let me tell you something very simple . . . this is a completely unrealistic, and completely false.

Unless you are demisexual and only feel attracted to those you have created mental or emotional bonds with, you will always feel attracted to other people, EVEN in loving relationships. This is simply the nature of being a sexual being.

For sexual beings, being attracted to others is a normal way of life—whether it is that toned guy with the infectious smile at the Deli, the girl with the attractive dress and alluring perfume at work, or the neighbor with the charming personality and hysterical jokes. Feeling attracted to other people does not make you evil, it does not make you a philanderer, and it does not make you guilty of a terrible crime.

But what does count is... **what you decide to do with these feelings**.

It's normal to feel attracted to other people while being in a committed relationship. However, you should not follow up on that fleeting desire. You should not act on those feelings. On the off chance that you truly need to follow up on your fascination towards another person, something is absent from your relationship. Your necessities are not being met in your present relationship so you are looking for that from outside.

Find your needs that are not being met. Discuss those requirements with your partner and make it so you needn't bother with anything from outside. You satisfy every one of your needs from your own relationship.

PART 2: Pitfalls to Avoid

CHAPTER 8

If Any Topic Comes Up Repeatedly, Take It Seriously

It's clear that relationship conflict occurs because expectations aren't being met. Each person comes into a relationship with certain expectations. These are based on past experiences, childhood, or how you think relationship should be.

If your partner is bringing up a topic repeatedly, pay attention. That is serious. If it was not, it wouldn't be brought up again. It may sound like a joke to you, but maybe it is serious for your partner.

The problem is that no two people think the same, no matter how much you have in common.

A lot of couples see disagreement as a time to bail - either because they were already looking for a way out or because they freak out and feel threatened. When our ego feels threatened, it activates our flight or fight response. Sometimes it may be hard to get resolution on a conflict, making matters worse.

Instead of seeing complains as a threat to a relationship, what if we reframed this and saw it as an opportunity and a sign of growth in a relationship?

This requires understanding that conflict will inevitably occur in a close relationship. The only way of getting around it is to not share your opinion at all, which is not healthy.

So what if we focused on sharing our opinions in a way that is productive?

To do this:

1. Remember not to sweat the small stuff.

Instead of making every little molehill a mountain, agree to not make something a battle unless it's truly important. Realize that not every disagreement needs to be an argument. Of course, this doesn't mean you bow to someone else's demands when it's something you feel strongly about but take the time to question the level of importance of the matter at hand.

2. Practice acceptance.

If you find yourself in the midst of a conflict, try to remember that the other person is coming into the situation with a totally different background and set of experiences than yourself. You have not been in this person's shoes, and while it may help to try to put yourself in them, your partner is the only person who can really explain where he or she is coming from.

3. Exercise patience.

Granted, it's hard to remember this in the heat of the moment. But stopping to take a few deep breaths, and deciding to take a break and revisit the discussion when tensions are not as high, can sometimes be the best way to deal with the immediate situation.

4. Lower your expectations.

This is not to say you should have low expectations but it is to say that you should keep in mind you may have different expectations. The best way to clarify this is to ask what their expectations are in a scenario. Again, don't automatically assume that you come into the situation with the same expectations.

But what if you are in the heat of a conflict and you don't seem to be doing anything other than polarizing each other?

5. Remember you both desire harmony.

Most likely, you both want to get back on track and have a peaceful relationship. Also remember the feeling of connectedness that you want to feel.It's hard to feel threatened by someone when you see yourselves as interconnected and working towards the same result.

6. Focus on the behavior of the person and not their personal characteristics.

Personal attacks can be far more damaging and long-lasting. Talk about what behavior upset you instead of what is "wrong" with someone's personality. Criticize their behavior, not their personality. Disagree with what they are doing, not with who they are as a person.

7. Clarify what the person meant by their action, instead of what you perceived their action to mean.

Most of the time, your partner is not deliberately trying to hurt you, and getting hurt happened to be a byproduct of that action.

8. Keep in mind your objective is to solve the problem, rather than win the fight.

Resist the urge to be contrary just for that reason. Remember that it's better to be happy than right!

9. Accept the other person's response.

Once you have shared your feelings as to what a person's actions meant to you, accept their responses. If they tell you the intended meaning of their action was not as you received it, take that as face value.

10. Leave it in the past.

Once you've both had the opportunity to share your side, mutually agree to let it go. Best case scenario, your discussion will end in a mutually satisfactory way. If it doesn't, you may choose to revisit it later. When making this decision, ask yourself how important it is to you. If you make the decision to leave it in the past, do your best to do that, rather than bringing it up again in future conflicts.

Conflict can be distressing. If you see it as an opportunity for growth, it can help you become closer and deepen your relationship.

CHAPTER 9

Let Sleeping Dogs Lie

One of the key elements of relationships is communication and using it effectively to deal with stuff that comes up. In this chapter, we will look at the importance of staying in the present as opposed to bringing up old stuff.

Storing things up

Many people somewhere along their upbringing have learnt that certain things should not be said and have, therefore, practiced storing things up. In a relationship these might be tiny things at the beginning: the fact that your partner leaves the toilet seat up, that the wet towel is on the floor every day, that her dirty knickers are on the floor in the bedroom or that he didn't let you know that he'll be home late. These little trivial things might not seem important enough to be mentioned in the moment but they might build up over time.

When do I need to say something?

At the beginning of a relationship we normally overlook things because we are filled up with 'in-love' hormones and see our partner through rose-colored glasses. 'He's my soul mate, we are perfect together' or 'she is different to any other girl I've met before' are sentences that are ripe with those hormones.

Sooner or later reality will set in and those rose-colored glasses will come off. Stay true to yourself from the beginning and own your right to saying what is important to you, even if it seems trivial.

Ask yourself: what is truly important to you? If you continue thinking about those little things and continuously get annoyed it is a sign that they are important to you and that you better bring it up before things get worse.

Deal with it now

If you have been in a relationship for a while you will have experienced those moments when you discuss things that annoy you or situations that you want changed. It is important that you stay present with what is happening right now.

Gathering ammunition in a fight by bringing up old stuff from last week, month or the past years is unfair and does not help your relationship. On the contrary, it creates defensiveness and confusion about what's the real issue.

Stay present

Make it your commitment in a relationship to regularly empty out current issues. Stop living in the past. Focus on staying present and deal with things that just occurred.

Remember that according to relationship expert Dr. John Gottman, 67% of the issues we face in relationship are perpetual issues. This means that we won't be able to find solutions in all the problems we are facing but masters of relationship are able to continuously communicate about those things with acceptance of the differences. By the way: you don't have to agree to everything but you have to at least accept your partner's choices.

Most of the time, it is better to accept that your opinion is different than the opinion of your partner on a perticular subject. It's fine. Just accept this fact and move on.

CHAPTER 10

The Role Of Bad Habits

I've got a dark secret habits. No, I'll take it back. I've got a couple of them. I keep them hidden from view, but sometimes people find out about them. I try to keep them hidden from sight as best I can. Listen, tell me how many addictions can you think of? I bet you can make a list and I bet it would be big.

I can think of a few. Here's some for starters: an addiction to drugs, an addiction to alcohol, a smoking addiction, a morally bad addiction, an addiction to gambling, an addiction to all the fattening foods that I can think about. Now, that's just a small list, but I'm sure there's many more that we can add to that list. When you have a relationship with someone, your bad habits affect that relationship. Period.

Many marriages and relationships are hurt by someone else's addiction.

Bad habits don't appear bad at first encounter. The first greasy burger, the first inhale from smoking pot, the first snort of cocaine, the first cigarette, the first drink, the first time you cheated on your mate, the first gambling session, the first lie, or the first time you yelled at the kids.

The first time you still feel in control. Even the second time is not so bad. But the compulsion quickly takes over especially if the stimulus has highly addictive qualities. When this happens, even though the mind may want to say "no", the body's addiction holds you hostage to the habit.

Identifying Unhealthy Habits

The first step in breaking bad habits is to identify them. I mentioned certain specific habits above but negative habits can also come in other forms. For example, you may have a habit of criticizing others or gossiping. You may be a constant worrier suffering from severe anxiety and insomnia. You may be a compulsive shopper and financially irresponsible. Whatever the habit, you must first seek to identify it.

There are times when it can be difficult to identify our bad habits. As human beings we tend to associate with people who support our habits. By doing so, the guilt and shame of the habit is disguised. Before long, the unhealthy habit begins to define you. You become known as the sex addict, or the television junkie, or the obese one. Look at yourself in the mirror and be honest with yourself. Identifying your bad habits is a form of acceptance of your habit, which is the first step toward kicking it.

So can you identify your unhealthy habits? Many of you are already aware what they are. When I had had a problem with negative thinking, the following were things I asked myself:

Is (fill in this space with the bad habit) holding me back from achieving my goal(s)?

Does (fill in this space with the bad habit) make me feel good about myself?

Is (fill in this space with the bad habit) something I feel proud of?

Is (fill in this space with the bad habit) something I feel comfortable doing in the open around my friends and family without causing me embarrassment?

Is (fill in this space with the bad habit) something I would encourage my child to do?

Do I listen to the advice of loved ones when they identify my negative habits or do I get on the defensive?

Begin today to identify your bad habits. If you are having difficulty, find a professional who can help you. Before long you will be able take back your life and accomplish all the goals you have set for you.

Examine Your Bad Habits

Once you have identified your bad habits, it's time to examine them to see how they affect your life and relationships. There are certain things to look for when examining these habits.

1. Examine how much time and effort goes into this habit. This helps you realize the severity of your habit. Think about how many years you have been stuck in this habit. Start to monitor your time by keeping a daily log of how much time you are engaged in this habit.

For example, if your habit is to sit and watch TV for hours, add up the amount of hours spent in front of the TV. Add it all up - the number of hours per day, per month, per year, times the number of years. Use this knowledge to become aware of how much of your precious time is wasted and how much control the television has over your life.

2. Examine how much money is spent on your habit. Make a conscious effort to log the amount of money you spend daily on you habit. For example, if your habit is drinking alcohol, add up how much you spend at the bars, or at the liquor store on a daily basis. Add it up at the end of the week and multiply it by the number of months or years you are stuck in this habit. Become

aware of how your hard earned dollar is wasted by your bad habit.

3. Examine your motive for indulging in your habit. For example, if your habit is drinking, look inside to see what it is you are trying to numb. Is it a bad relationship, or a painful childhood, or some type of emotional trauma? If you cannot identify the motive, you must seek professional guidance to get to the core reason of your habit and resolve it.

4. Examine the effects of your habit. How is it hurting your health, your spouse, your family, or your relationships? Are you putting your job in jeopardy? Is your bad habit causing you to put off doing important things in your life? Is it affecting your ability to think clearly? Is it getting in the way of achieving your goals?

It is then important to accept that you should control your behaviors instead of trying to control others. Make it a habit to be proactive instead of reactive. Reactive behavior can lead to defensiveness and can allow a simple phrase or a missed gesture to negate the best of rapport or spontaneity. Proactive behavior helps you to remain in control of what you say and of what you do.

Recognizing & adjusting your behavior helps you to avoid misunderstanding, discomfort, and conflict.

CHAPTER 11

How Money Problems Affect Your Relationships?

There are a lot of households stressed about money these days. Financial crisis has couples and families of all ages worried. Some fear paying bills, others worry about retirement as they see their savings dwindle. It is often hard to keep the stress and worry from affecting marriages.

Due to constant fear & worry, we often find it hard to be nicer to the ones we love. Here are some suggestions for couples who who are undergoing tough times:

1. Acknowledge that this is a tough time. Do not deny the seriousness of the situation. Talk together about your worries, fears, anger and sadness. Expressing your thoughts calm you down and builds trust with your partner.

2. Don't blame the past. What's done cannot be undone. Don't look back. While you did not get here over night, it is highly likely that neither of you anticipated what has happened with the economy. Just learn from the past and let it go.

3. Pointing fingers at the past does not help, although discovering what to do differently can be very helpful. It is possible that one of you may have been more of a spender, maybe even significantly more of a spender, however you cannot change the past. Look to and plan for the present and the future.

3. Remember that you are on the same team. Even in tough times, both of you have the same desire, to resolve the problematic situation. Think of this as a puzzle to figure out together. View each other as a team-mate, not an opponent. Talk with each other in ways that promote encouragement and good feelings.

4. Share the burden. Do not try to solve the problem all alone. Sharing makes it easier to cope up with difficult times. Ask your spouse to handle the bills every other month or be in charge of making sure unwanted lights are put out, clip coupons, walk to the store, etc. Think together about how you can help each other as you look for ways to survive and then thrive.

5. Plan regular "financial summits". Plan to meet on a regular basis to talk about money, budgets and bills. Use actual facts and figures to plot your moves. Try to find a way to make them a little less stressful like pouring a cup of coffee and sitting on the back deck or going to McDonalds for ice cream and talking it over away from home. However you do it, though, make sure that you both do it and are open, honest and "scratching your heads" together over how to handle the money.

6. Make goals. A small percentage in savings? Stretching the paycheck to last throughout the pay period? Paying off one credit card? Monitor you progress on the goal and scratch them off when you have been successful.

7. Try to keep things as normal as possible. Have date nights and family nights even if you have to be very frugal. An inexpensive date could be walking together at the beach during sunset. Surprisingly, some of the best things in life need little to no money.

8. Make sure to have fun with each other and promote laughter and play. The more you can generate positive times and put

deposits in the emotional bank account, the easier it will be to get through the tough times and difficult decisions.

9. Celebrate the goodness of your relationship. While you will need to spend regular time thinking and talking about the money, remember and focus on the good things in your lives and in each other. Be grateful for what you have. Ask yourself, "what is good in my life right now?" Remind each other about the good things you have going for you and be grateful for it.

If you wish to know more about gratitude, I suggest my book "*Gratitude: Getting in touch with what really matters*"

CHAPTER 12

Impact of Health Problems on Your Relationship

From my perspective, one of the most important piece affecting our relationships with our loved ones is our physical health.

It is mostly determined by our life style. This involves our daily diet and our daily activity or the lack there of. If we don't have righteous thinking and discipline, our physical health will suffer dramatically.

If we don't live a healthy life style, then we are going to age quickly with poor health physically and mentally. We have to maintain a healthy body & mind in order to be happy and our happiness determines how well we relate to our loved ones.

Our body speaks to us 24/7, 365 days a year but we don't listen. If you feel an ache, feel sluggish, feel lack of energy and if you are a little heavier than you would like to be, don't ignore what your body is saying to you. pay attention and do something about it. Our outlook in life is more positive and more 'God like' when we are feeling good. As we become more negative about life because of our physical health, we become less God like.

It is a snowball effect in that our physical health affects our mental health, which in turns affects our spiritual health. All of this has an effect on our relationship with our loved ones.

If we are feeling good about ourselves, then we are going to be more caring and compassionate with our spouses, family and friends. Aside from personal and employment issues, our mental state is closely related to our physical state. So, it benefits us to make every effort to stay healthy physically and mentally.

Our physical and mental health will help us deal better with any stressful situation that may arise from our daily interactions. Keep in mind that time is not on your side because if you are procrastinating as to when you are going to start some form of exercise and make changes in your life style, you are kidding yourself.

The longer you put off getting your body and mind in shape, the worse your situation is going to get. The healthier you are mentally, the healthier you will be in your daily interactions.

For the love of God, anyone who is reading this book, if you are active physically, mentally and spiritually, please continue to do so and if you are not active physically and mentally, do yourself a favor and become more active because you don't want to be less than optimum physically and mentally in your golden years. Do this for yourself and for your loved ones. The culmination of your physical and mental health is your spiritual health.

This God-like state of mind is what allows you to live a wonderful life. A life that is full of love, caring, and compassion is a spiritual life.

This is what Jesus teaching was all about. It is the feeling of loving life, respecting life, treating everyone and every living being with reverence that makes us a spiritual being in the likeness of our creator.

It makes no difference whether you attend a house of prayer on a weekly basis or not as long as you meditate/pray in your secret place (the kingdom within) and keep a constant relationship with God in your own way. Your spiritual health plays a big part in your relationship with your spouse, your children, your friends and your community.

CHAPTER 13

Never Take Relationships For Granted

There is a point in most relationships when one or both of the partners begin to take each other for granted. They stop worrying about how they look around the other person, how they act around the other person, and even stop caring so much about how that other person is feeling.

Sometimes this happens when people just start being committed to each other and very often this happens few months after the wedding. That's where the term "the honeymoon's over" comes from. That is the point where people have started to take their partner for granted. We'll listen up guys (and gals) because we are going to cover how to avoid this trap, and if you're already in it, how to get out of it. So you can see why finding cute names to call your girlfriend is merely the beginning in forming a strong bond with your mate.

First off I want to explain to you why it's so important to not take your partner for granted. You see, people get attracted to you when you are actively applying the power inside of you to win their love and affection. While they may stay in the relationship with you for years or even decades when you don't win their love, they are only doing it out of obligation or possibly because you have children together. As soon as you think that you "have" that person and that they are not going to go anywhere you begin to lose ground and that person begins to lose attraction to you.

You must, and I repeat, MUST win that person's attention, affection and love. Both Men and women must participate equally in this practice to have a happy relationship.

Here's the real, simple, secret to having a great life together: *Treat each other as if neither one of you has any obligation to be with the other.*

Understand that true happiness comes from constantly having the same attraction to each other as you did when you were first dating. Start to GIVE to that other person in every way you can, and START NOW! So where do you start?

You have to begin to develop yourself into the best version of yourself as possible, while also increasing your knowledge of attraction and what will best attract your partner to you. Strive to be "excellent", as the zen master would say. You must learn the secrets of magnetic attraction to create and unbreakable bond between you and your partner.

CHAPTER 14

Dealing With A Broken Heart

Whether it comes out of the blue or is something you've been anticipating, being dumped is rarely pleasant. While for some people it might come as a relief, or be part of an amicable separation; for most the shock and distress that comes from rejection can be difficult to cope with. This applies whether it's a romantic relationship break-up, losing a friend, or family estrangement.

Although a cliché, the idea that 'the only way through it is through it' applies here. However there are things you might consider to make the process easier to cope with. Getting over loss takes time and may be affected by several factors.

It's common to fixate on the past relationship – dissecting why it went 'wrong', or planning how to repair it, and to be preoccupied with memories of your relationship (good or bad). You may want to do anything to get your ex back, or may accept the relationship is over but still feel upset. Not being part of your ex's life could make you feel disoriented and lonely.

These responses may vary in intensity and last for weeks, months or longer. They may be consistently present or flare up intermittently.

These feelings may seem beyond your control, which can be distressing. Generally you would expect negative and sad feelings to reduce over time, although there is no set period in which everyone should recover from a break-up.

How not to cope with a break-up?

Standard advice says using drugs or alcohol to numb the pain of a break-up is wrong, yet many people temporarily do this as a coping strategy. If you find alcohol/drugs are causing problems you may wish to seek professional help.

Being fixated with your ex is common when a relationship ends. If this moves into consistent, repeated, unwanted contact with your ex, their family, friends or workmates, this is stalking. If you are very angry or distressed, talk to friends or family, ask your GP for help or refer yourself to a counselor rather than engaging in revenge behaviours where you try and harm your ex's reputation, emotional well-being, or physical health.

Ways to help yourself after a break-up

We all experience break-ups differently. There is no 'right' coping strategy.

Acknowledge the feelings you have. We're led to feel there are correct, sanitized ways to manage a break-up where we must be reasonable and responsible. Behind the scenes, you may wish to rage, cry and rant about what has happened. While living with emotional pain is distressing, some people find it cathartic or a necessary way to acknowledge their upset at losing something important.

Self care may seem obvious but try to eat, rest and relax. If you have lost your appetite, small snacks may suit you better than big meals. If you're not sleeping at night, try to nap in the day or at least try and rest while you are awake may be useful.

If friends/family want to help, ask them for practical support like doing shopping, housework, cooking or childcare. Or just to be there to listen to you if you need to talk, cry or need distracting.

Don't assume all break-ups have to end with hostility. It's easy to get caught into a trap of seeing yourself as the good guy and your ex as the baddy. While they may have hurt you, they will have their own view about what has happened and may also be struggling with the split.

If the break-up has left you feeling suicidal speak to your GP, go to A&E or call The Samaritans. If you have existing or past mental health problems you may want to speak to your GP if the break-up is causing you additional distress.

Dating again?

Part of our culture's post break up story is we'll be sure to find love again. Literature, films and love songs tell about the happier future that awaits us with a new love. However this isn't what happens for all of us – and nor is it what everyone desires.

It may be you don't want to consider another relationship if you are struggling with grief, confidence issues or other worries. The practical aspects of managing a separation (particularly if you have dependants) may take up a lot of your time.

Alternatively, you may want a break from dating if you've been in a series of relationships that keep ending and it's leaving you distressed.

There is no set period of post break-up mourning to observe. However, and some people find themselves in a new relationship quickly while others wait awhile – by choice or due to other factors.

This will pass

Over time the feelings of loss, despair and heartbreak should recede. Although it may feel impossible to believe when you are in the grips of misery and the stomach churning realization of loss.

There is no set time for this to happen. More likely you'll find there just is a day when life isn't quite so hard, or when you start looking back and wondering why you were so upset. Or when you no longer think about your ex at all.

We're encouraged to see relationship breakdown as a disaster. It may be more helpful to see it as a change, a chance for personal growth, and the opportunity for things to be different. Repeating this to ourselves along with the coping strategies listed above may seem like small gestures but they can be empowering. As can knowing things should get better in time, and if they don't there are people around to help.

If you are dealing with breakup, I suggest checking out my book "*Forgiveness: The greatest cure for a suffering heart*"

CHAPTER 15

The War For Control

Do you often feel overwhelmed or smothered by the man you are with? How much level of control should each partner have in a relationship? If you tend to lose control in relationships, keep reading for important information about how to balance things out.

Every relationship must have boundaries no matter how much the two of you love each other. There is a fine balance between making sacrifices for the best interest of your relationship and losing yourself in another person entirely. A loving partner should never require you to give up your life in order to accommodate him. Doing so almost always leads to resentment in a relationship.

Additionally, when you give up all control, your partner will begin to take you for granted. Don't give up control just to avoid conflict. Conflicts can be resolved, but control is very hard to regain once you give it away.

The power to be in control in a relationship needs to be shared by both parties involved. It should truly be a partnership where each person is giving an equal amount of effort.

It is okay to say 'no' to unreasonable requests from your partner. Just be sure to explain your position so they understand where you are coming from. And remember that it is a two way street. He is also free to say 'no' if he feels you are making unreasonable demands. Being in control of your relationship can feel like an unpleasant topic, but it is critically important that you and your partner find common ground in this area.

CHAPTER 16

The Fear Of Loosing Your Partner

Too many people sabotage their dating life and their romantic relationships because their thoughts and actions in a relationship are paralyzed by their fear of loss of that relationship. They treat their relationship like some kind of precious, gentle egg shell that must be preserved and protected at any cost, and many of their actions in a relationship are governed by that fear of loss in a relationship.

If you are one of those people who is really afraid that your partner will leave you, cheat on you, stop loving you, break up with you or otherwise slip away, you should be aware of one very important truth: your fear is both pointless and harmful!

You have to realize and remember that there is no point in worrying about things that are simply not in your control. It so happens that there is no insurance policy against breaking up and losing your loved one. People break up and divorce after 10 or more years of being together, so it's important to realize and accept that that risk is always there.

Fear of loss is very similar to jealousy in that it suffocates the other person, so to speak. It makes him/her that tremendous pressure of being the most important thing in your life and being the "gauge" of your happiness. Ironically, then, the more afraid you are to lose your lover, the more your actions will push him/her away from you.

It is important, therefore, to liberate yourself of this fear if you want to enjoy a good relationship and be a good partner. Here are a few steps that you can and should take in order to let go of this fear of losing your partner:

1. Realize and remember that your partner's actions in the future are out of your hands.

Your partner's actions and his/her being or not being faithful don't just depend on you and therefore you should not feel responsible for them. Accept the fact that it's possible that your partner will leave one day.

While you should focus on the positive and assume the best about your partner and about your relationship until and unless proven otherwise, the reality is that there is no insurance policy against sudden and unexpected break-ups or other bad news in a relationship. This is just part of being involved in a relationship.

2. Make sure that you do your part by doing what depends on you.

While, as noted above, how your partner behaves doesn't wholly depend on you, your actions and what you bring to the table in a relationship is of course a major factor. Jealousy, being controlling, and watching your partner's every step is one of the common reasons for both break-ups and infidelity. If you suffocate your partner by being jealous, controlling and overbearing, it's only natural that he will start looking sooner or later to have more freedom alone or with someone else who allows him to have more freedom.

A more free life, free of close supervision and micromanagement on the part of your partner, is a better life and that's what anyone who feels being under the microscope will be seeking.

3. Realize that even if you lose that very special person in your life, it's not going to be the end of the world.

You will survive that loss if you end up breaking up with your partner, and you will move forward. It might be hard for you to believe, but there is life out there after your partner leaves you, whether you are able to believe it today or not. This doesn't mean that you should prepare yourself for your relationship to be over, but it's a good idea to be realistic and simply know that it's always a possibility.

So, stop letting the fear of loss in a relationship dictate your behavior and actions. Be the best partner you can be and leave the rest to the greater good to determine where your relationship will go. And if you end up breaking up for some petty reason, it's a pretty strong sign that it would not have been the right person for you anyway, and it's a blessing that you found this out sooner than later. After all, if you both feel strongly about each other, petty things should only be causing arguments and fights; not a break-up.

Don't Let Your Past Affect Your New Relationship

Going through bad relationships is part of life and part of our growth. Yet, the hurt that remains seem to create a hole in our hearts and affect our trust & faith in finding true, lasting relationships.

The question that I'd love to invite you to reflect on is: What have been the consequences of what you believe about your past relationships, yourself, and life? If we look around, we will see that many people have probably suffered more than we have. It may not be in relationships but it different forms. Pain is universal and heartache is the same no matter what form it takes.

I am not saying this to devalue our pain or our experiences. I am saying this because human beings do suffer, but they often suffer more as a result of their thoughts and the stories they tell themselves than from what actually happened to them. When we dwell on the past and when allow our fear of being hurt again, rejected and abandoned to control our lives, we sabotage every possible opportunity we have towards love and finding a beautiful relationships.

Sometimes, we use our bad experiences to protect ourselves from leaving our comfort zone or to feed our human need for love, connection, wholeness, certainty, and significance. As humans, our mind conditions us to believe that we must fix our past and be perfect to be happy; we can only earn this happiness when have the validation and certainty that we will never be hurt again.

However, I came to learn that pain can't be avoided. The more we push it away, the more we attract it and experience it because we're fighting against our reality. But, it is not what happens to us that shapes our relationships; it is what we do about what happens and the way we perceive it. There is a difference between feeling like a victim of life and fighting to get love versus allowing love to come through us and towards us and finding the silver lining behind our experiences. It's all about perception and the question here: are we brave enough to sit with this pain, look through it and come back to our source which is "love?"

Love is the source to life and it is available to each one of us. It doesn't have a barrier except for the stories that we create. It is right here ready to welcome us back into a beautiful relationship when we're ready to take the risk of shattering old patterns that have kept it from speaking through us and coming towards us. I believe that true love is much closer to us than our own breath.The key to attracting a long lasting relationship is to change our beliefs and stories about our past and about ourselves. Do you deserve true love? Of course you do. We all do.

Stop protecting yourself from pain and decide to reveal the love that you are regardless of what's in store for you. Trust that your past experience is bringing you one step closer to being with someone who deserves you and that a higher power above is guiding you way.

CHAPTER 17

Small Mistakes Can Harm A Relationship

You think that he or she is someone you really see yourself committing to, with a serious relationship seeming just right around the corner.

This is how most people start dating. However, before taking things ahead, it is essential to realize that two different individuals will have their own set of opinions and qualities. Sure, there are going to be arguments and discussions, but this is natural in relationships.

An important thing to remember before entering in a serious relationship is imbibing the quality of empathy in yourself first. Settling any issue would be easy if you start respecting your partner's opinions. Just feeling strongly about something does not make you right and your partner wrong. There are always two sides of a coin, and if you really want to make your relationship work, you need to avoid common mistakes that can destroy it.

Bottling up Emotions

Members of both sexes face this problem. There are certain things about your partner that you certainly don't appreciate, and do want to change. You want to talk about it and clear your mind, but instead of solving the problem, you hold it in. This may act as a temporary solution, but this isn't a passing phase, and might prove quite unhealthy in the long-run. Such bottling up of emotions can increase negativity, frustration, distance, and create problems between the two of you.

Taking for Granted

This is something that most individuals do when they have been together for some time. Sure, for your spouse, you are always perfect, but he or she definitely cares about the way you look. What happened to that gorgeous woman? Or where did that handsome guy suddenly vanish? Remember, just because you are finally with the one you desire, you can't become lax about your appearance and habits. Putting in the effort to present yourself better is an investment likely to give the best returns.

The Ex-Factor

If you are still hung up on your ex, then it isn't healthy to rush into a new relationship, as it can have devastating consequences. Many times, just to make their 'ex' jealous, people try to appear extremely confident and happy with their new squeeze.

First of all, never enter a relationship just to show-off in front of your ex. In time, you will start comparing your present with the past, resulting in a pretty nasty situation.

Not Listening

One of the most common mistakes that ends a relationship is not listening to the other person. We all believe ourselves to be good listeners, but watching TV, playing with your phone, checking email, or even thinking of something else while the other person is talking is termed as not listening. When you don't pay attention to what the other person is saying, it disrupts the bond between you two, causing a communication gap that drifts you apart.

Preset Expectations

Idealizing your relationship, life, and partner is a sure shot way to ruin your relationship. You start imagining your partner in a new avatar, but that isn't reality. Gradually you come to terms with the truth, but feel dissatisfied and start blaming yourself or your partner. Remember this, there is always scope for improvement in a relationship, and there is no such thing as a perfect relationship or a perfect partner.

Infidelity

This point is essential for both men and women. Betrayal can never be tolerated, be it emotional or physical. Once the deed has been done, your relationship is never going to be the same again. Gaining your spouse's trust again can be extremely difficult, so think twice before crossing the line.

Being Extra Nice

Avoid dressing up in gorgeous lingerie or buying her expensive items frequently. It is really nice that you want to make your spouse feel special, but these frequent surprises will just look like you are trying too hard to impress.

Your spouse might feel bad, and start looking out for ways to compensate for these special treats. It is great if you do nice things for each other from time to time, but don't escalate into a panic mode and start doing it every day.

Always Defensive

It is normal for individuals to get into a defensive mode when questioned or criticized by their spouse. They also try to justify their behavior and mistakes, instead of admitting to their wrongdoing. Also, constant expectations and complaints make matters worse, and can permanently damage your relationship. In a happy and content relationship, mistakes are accepted on both sides, and serious efforts are taken to make amends.

Mental or Physical Abuse

There is no place for abuse in love. Be it mental or physical abuse, it is wrong, and quite unhealthy for both. There are many cases where abuse has often been mistaken for genuine concern or possessiveness. It may seem like your partner really cares, but any signs of over-possessiveness, excessive jealousy, and a controlling attitude are not indicative of genuine affection. A healthy relationship involves mutual respect, love, and commitment.

Lack of Intimacy

Not surprisingly, lack of intimacy has caused many relationships to end. Whether physical or emotional, intimacy is extremely essential for any relationship to flourish. Also remember that you need to have a perfect mixture of physical and emotional intimacy. This can't be expressed in just plain words; you need to put in feelings and that extra dose of love to make it special. It is intimacy which acts as a foundation through tough times and helps you realize the value of love and togetherness.

Relationships requires commitment and are fragile in nature. Every couple goes through difficult times, but that does not mean they should split up. Just try to avoid these common errors of judgment and you'll be fine.

PART 3: Creating a Fulfilling Relationship

CHAPTER 18

Be Open With Your Partner

Some people are instinctively honest and open; some would say that these people are too open and trusting and in this way leave themselves open and vulnerable to others.

Some people are more guarded and watch what they say and do around others and either keep themselves to themselves or only show a selective view of themselves to others; in this way they both protect themselves and avoid conflict.

What is the best way for someone to be? It is inevitable that there are both benefits and detriments to both angles. There is a flip side to every coin. I cannot help but think that in the long run it must be better overall to be yourself and show the real you, the authentic self, to others. Sometimes you may be ribbed or taken advantage of, or have to deal with conflicts, but it is quite simply easier to be yourself and therefore easier to build comfortable and "real" relationships.

As you get older and have more experience you learn who to trust with your innermost thoughts and who not to. As we build confidence and self-esteem we trust our instincts more and automatically adapt our own behavior to suit the circumstances. Sometimes though, if you have not been exposed to the most nurturing circumstances you will have erected a wall which you hide the real you behind. This makes sense as your instinct of survival tells you that you should protect yourself from danger.

The downside of this instinctive protective measure is that you cut yourself off from creating close ties with others; you stop yourself from developing deep friendships and relationships. This, in turn, has the effect of knocking your self-esteem still further and promoting feelings of depression. Human beings are sociable creatures; we need contact and interaction with others to feel at our best. The quality and quantity of social interaction is linked to our sense of self.

A recent study into the behavior of young girls by Sally Theran, assistant professor of psychology at Wellesley College, supports the premise that being open and honest promotes the building of closer bonds and also greater happiness in life. (Sally A Theran. "Authenticity with Authority Figures and Peers: Girls' Friendships, Self-Esteem, and Depressive Symptomatology," The Journal of Social and Personal Relationships, June 2010)

We are happier when we have a high sense of self-worth and self-esteem. We are happier when we are involved in close and meaningful relationships. If we guard our thoughts and feelings too protectively, whilst we do stop ourselves from immediate hurt and conflict but we at the same time run the risk of hurting ourselves more deeply in the long term, as we cannot build the best of relationships without being open and honest. If you are not your authentic self you are more likely to suffer loss of self-esteem, depression and unhappiness.

CHAPTER 19

Express Your Love

One of the most prestigious gifts of God to humans is Love. We can't live without Love. Love makes our Life more beautiful and worth living. When we fall in love, everything seems to be great. We feel like that the whole world has fallen beneath our feet and we are the happiest person in the world.

Love is a beautiful feeling and you need to express it to your beloved. You can't have a long term relationship without expressing your love time to time. You can make good impression on your beloved by learning different ways of expressing Love. So here are some ways to express your feelings of Love:

1. First of all, we should always express our feelings to our partner by using words. I love you, I like it when you do that, I really appreciate this about you and so on. Normally, we forget the importance of affectionate words in relationship. We think we are past that stage. Wrong. You are never past expressing your love to your partner. It is the foundation of healthy relationships.

2. One of the best ways to put your love feelings in words is through writing. It is very popular method amongst lovers to express Love. Even a short note saying "I love you very much", "I am thinking about you", "I am missing and I can't live without you" work like magic.

Surprising each other like this is one of the best ways to express your love Feelings and to strengthen your bond.

3- As discussed earlier, touch is one of the most important parts of love. It is capable to express your love towards each other. When you are walking on the road, in the park or everywhere, you can hold each other's hand. It can be quite beneficial to your relationship. Hugging each other, walking together, hand shake, holding hands are quite a nice ways to express your Love.

4- Sending gifts to your beloved is another exotic way to express your feelings of love and of care. You can gift him or her Candles, Teddy Bear, Heart Shape or anything you like. It doesn't matter whether your gift is small or big, but it should be able to convey your feelings of Love towards your partner.

5- Frequently take break from your work and go to a vacation with your beloved. You can go to vacation on weekend or just for a day. Go to a place where you can get a different environment than usual. Just enjoy your vacation, relax and express your love for each other.

3- YouTube is a rather new and impressive way to express Love. YouTube is a video sharing website where everyone can upload his or her video and share with the whole. Create a video expressing your Love feelings towards your Beloved and then upload it t Youtube.

They'll give you a link where your video can be viewed. Send this Link to him/her via SMS and E-mail. Isn't a great way to express your Love? Of course, it is. So folks, create your video declaring your love and let the whole world know how much you love him or her.

Use the above five ways to tell your beloved how much you love him/her and how much you care for him/her. It will certainly spice up your love life and makes your relationship more romantic.

CHAPTER 20

Importance Of Special Time Together

Spending time together with your spouse or loved one can take a back seat once you grow comfortable in the marriage or relationship. Learning to sustain your marriage and follow relationship advice will assist you in creating and nurturing your relationships to a level where it can sustain difficult times. The most important aspect in any relationship is to make time for one another. Try out these few key ideas to learn how you can make more quality time for your spouse.

Schedule a weekend once a month to spend time with your loved one. Having the chance to be alone and just the two of you to interact without the distractions of the outside world will give you an opportunity to reconnect on a regular and consistent basis. As you become more involved with your spouse or partner, you both to grow together as a couple.

Some couples may find it difficult to take out a full weekend just for the two of them every month if they have extreme work schedules or children they are caring for. If this is the scenario for you, talk to your spouse and ask for suggestions or ideas of how you can find more time to spend together alone. You may discover that you can set aside one evening a week or one weekend morning every weekend to be together.

Relationship advice suggests that you do creative and enjoyable things together in addition to simply making time for conversation. Consider in enrolling in a cooking class or painting class together. If this does not suit you, there are many other options you both can explore together.

You may find that a hiking trip once every other week will satisfy and stimulate your relationship, or you may discover that you would both like to take a sculpting class together.

Making a conscious decision to pursue more quality time together as a couple will lead you down a road of enlightenment in your relationship. You will both gain more wisdom about one another and more experience in communication and in keeping your priorities straight.

Too many couples allow their feelings for one another to grow dim and for the fire that once burned brightly between them to wan down to embers. You no longer have to settle for this if this has begun to happen to your marriage or relationship. This is a common activity in marriages and relationships and one that can be reversed with commitment and effort.

Comprehensive and realistic relationship advice will help you to turn the current situation around and to make more time for one another so that your relationship can bloom and flourish under the nurturing you give it. When you plan your time to spend alone together, remember to plan something romantic and something that each of you will enjoy and benefit from so that it will be a special and memorable experience you both will want to repeat often.

CHAPTER 21

The Importance Of Eye Contact

What is eye contact?

Several popular definitions are:

1. Eye contact is one of the most important nonverbal channels you have for communicating and connecting with others.

2. Defined as a meeting of the eyes between two people expresses meaningful nonverbal communication.

3. Contact that occurs when two people look directly at each other at the same time.

4. It is the condition or action of looking another human in the eye.

Linda Eve Diamond:

"The cheapest, most effective way to connect with people is to look them in the eye."

What does it do?

Eye Contact can trigger:

Fighting

Smiling

Acknowledgment

love

Understanding

Encouragement

Eye meeting is two souls touching. Imagine, all the power your eyes hold.

Of all the ways we communicate, eye contact maybe the most powerful.The first step in establishing communication is eye contact.

Communication with pets and animals is with eye contact, and depending on the animal you maintain or avoid contact.

Did you ever look at a horse and know that your souls had communicated?

Have you ever looked at your dog and known that the two of you connected at a spiritual level?

My best friend and I can communicate volumes with just a glance.

So are the eyes a window to the soul? I'd say so.

What is the power of making contact with the eyes?

Ralph Waldo Emerson:

"*An eye can threaten like a loaded gun, or it can insult like hissing or kicking or in its altered mood, be a beam of kindness. It can make the heart dance for joy.*"

Words will probably never be found to communicate what actually transpires when you are communicating with another living creature through eye contact. Maybe it should it be "I" contact?

Besides touch, the eyes are the most powerful way of delivering personal cues.

Eyes show personal involvement and creates intimate bonds. Mutual gazing narrows physical gaps. It brings people closer. The eyes play an indispensable role in effective communication and the building relationships.

The look of love; remember that look and the physical wham when wordlessly you knew you were attracted.

What can you say with the eyes?

When you make contact it says to the other person:

I am interested in you

I respect you

I trust you

You have my attention

I value you

Our eyes are wonderful gifts. They help us express our feelings of love, acceptance, hope, warning, fear, anger and much more, without a word.

CHAPTER 22

Touch Builds Intimacy

If you long to hear the words, "I love you," you'll be surprised to learn that touching is what will catapult your relationship into the intimacy you desire. You see words are processed in the thinking part of your brain whereas touch goes directly to your emotional centers. Read on to learn 5 fantastic ways to touch.

Touching is one of the most intimate of all actions. It allows you to move into sacred space, creating presence and connection. And yet, we are a touch starved society.

A study done in the 1960's showed the drastic differences in cultures by observing how many touches were exchanged with pairs of people around the world in coffee houses. Puerto Ricans got the prize touching 180 times an hour while Americans adhered to a strict diet touching only twice within an hour. The hunger for touch may manifest as depression, anxiety, irritability, boredom, pain, moodiness as well as make you feel isolated, separate and lonely.

Thus began some serious research on the importance of touch leading to the discovery that the amount of skin-to-skin contact in our lives plays a crucial role in our happiness and vitality. The act of touching influences our ability to form close relationships with other people, to deal with stress and pain, and even to fight off disease.

So many women complain that their relationships lack intimacy. We are born with an intense skin hunger. The emotional development of babies depends on tons of touching and as adults we have a strong need to be held in someone's arms, hold hands, be cuddled, be caressed, etc.

However, most people don't touch as often as they would like - afraid of being rejected, seen as needy or vulnerable they cover their need for intimacy with work, activities, TV food, drugs, alcohol.

The first step to developing a successful, intimate relationship with your partner is to first build intimacy with yourself. Exploring every delicious curve of your body will help you get to know what you like and what makes you feel good.

Once you've got this down, you can reach out to your partner with confidence and create the closeness you crave.

With all these fantastic reasons to bring touch into relationships, let's take alook at 5 ways you can incorporate touch into your life.

1) Create an intimate connection to yourself by putting on some soft tunes, lighting a candle, laying down, closing your eyes and letting you hands glide over your body, touching every delicious curve.

Enhance this exercise by using an aromatherapy lotion or essential oil with a sexy scent like ylang-ylang or rose. Feel your sense of sensual Self expand!

2) Hugging - full body hugging increases closeness, connection and safety.

3) Kissing - a 20 second kiss will raise his testosterone levels and make you feel closer

4) Massage

The shoulders, hands and feet get emotionally stimulated when touched. New York-based sex therapist Mildred Witkin, suggests couples should practice touching in a way that is not explicitly sexual to keep intimacy and playfulness alive.

5) Two to Tango: Dance classes are a great way to meet new people and have your hand and waist held all evening long. Contact your local YMCA or dance studio for schedules.

Follow these five steps to increase touching and you'll soon be building the connection and intimacy you crave.

CHAPTER 23

Listen Intently

Are you listening to me?" This is a common phrase heard between couples during a typical conversation.

On a larger scale, there are several cultures where people seem to talk all at the same time and you wonder if anyone is listening. It appears ridiculous to see two, three or more people talking at the same time to each other in a group. While it looks funny, there can be a communication lesson that can be learned here.

But more importantly, in a relationship constant communication is essential. In fact, it is vital not to keep on guessing what is in the mind of the other person. To build good listening skills in a relationship is a critical element in keeping communication open.

Everyone wants the other person to listen to him or her when he's doing the talking. But not everyone wants to listen. More often or not, we always have something to say and we like to look for an audience to listen to us.

However, being a good listener is not an accident. To build good listening skills in a relationship can be learned.

And being a good listener can make you a "great conversationalist" to your partner. This would add "spice" to the relationship and not make it boring. Learn to be an good active listener.

Here are some steps to become a good active listener:

1.Look at your partner when he or she is talking

This would give the impression that you are truly listening. Eye contact is crucial in active listening. Looking away or elsewhere gives the other a feeling that you are not interested in what he has to say.

2.Lean towards your spouse and listen intently

This action shows interest in what your spouse is saying. Body language, at times, says more than what you are actually saying. Smiling, and nodding in response encourages people to continue speaking, and it shows that your attention is focused on the conversation. Don't move around and say "Go ahead I'm listening" while you're fixing or working on something.

3.Save your comments at the end

While your spouse is speaking, don't butt in. You would not want that to happen to you. Much as you have good suggestions, save it at the end. Don't think what to say next because while you're thinking, you're not listening.

Another is jumping to another topic other than what your partner is saying. That will tell him or her that you are not interested in what he or she is saying. After he is done, say encouraging thoughts or suggestions and nothing negative.

4.Be patient when listening

Don't hurry up your spouse especially when he or she is excited to tell you a story, an experience or more so a problem. Sometimes we may have many things to do but it is very important that you put all these aside first and give all your attention to your spouse. This act of love is one way of showing that your spouse is important. He will also feel your love and will be very happy and appreciate you more.

These steps help in improving communication. To build good listening skills in a relationship especially with love will ensure a solid partnership. As stated earlier, improved communication between spouses or partners is key to having that relationship always fresh and exciting.

CHAPTER 24

Statements Of Affection

Giving your partner compliments when you are alone is wonderful for building appreciation and romantic affection. However, giving your partner compliments in the company of other people shows them how genuinely you respect and care for them openly within a social environment. Do this in creative and unique ways that makes other people appreciate the wonderful things you see within your partner on a daily basis.

As a rule-of-thumb, not only should you compliment your partner in a creative manner, you should also only compliment them on things that others simply would not at first notice. If for instance others see your partner as being handsome or beautiful, compliment them indirectly about how great of a husband, wife, father, mother or provider they are - this will show them beyond a shadow of a doubt how much you respect, care and value them.

Say "I Love You" in a Variety of Ways

Don't just say "I love you", instead say it differently, creatively and in a variety of ways. Here are few examples:

You complete me…

You are precious…

You are my life…

I value you…

I adore you…

You inspire me…

I live for our love…

You are my strength…

I dream of you…

I appreciate you…

Me and you always…

These are just some examples that you can use to tell your partner that you love them.

CHAPTER 25

The Significance Of Time And Date

In every relationship, there will be some dates that are special. It is a good idea to remember these dates to surprise your partner. Forgetting important dates can make a serious effect on your relationship, especially if you have a partner who gives more importance to it.

Remembering a date that has importance in your relationship can show how much you value the intimacy. You never forget your birthday, the day you got your first salary, the day when you received your first increment or your passport renewal date. It should be the same with your relationship and your partner. This will help you keep your relationship fresh with the fragrance of all those good days of the past.

Always remember the important dates. If you don't have a sharp memory, try other ways; like keeping a reminder in your phone, saving in your email calendar, writing down in your personal diary or including it in your 'to-do list'.

Your partner is waiting to see whether you remember all those special moments. Don't disappoint them. Here are some dates that you should never forget in a relationship:

1. Their Birthday:

No excuse can replace the frustration that you presented your partner by forgetting their birthday. Everybody who is in a relationship wants their partner to remember their birthday. Whether you gave a gift or not, it doesn't matter as much as remembering the date itself. Having the date in your mind shows that you care, rest of the things are secondary.

2. Your child's birthday:

There are many partners who are not so particular about remembering all those important dates. But, if you have a child, it is important to remember their date of birth. Considering this as one of the dates that you should never forget will make your partner happy.

3. Their mom's birthday:

Everybody wants their partner to love their mother as their own. Keep the date of birth of your mother-in-law in your memory as a date that you should never forget. Wish for her birthday and see how surprised your partner will be. You can try this with your other in-laws as well.

4. Anniversary:

The day when you both became one has great importance in your relationship, making it one of the important dates that you should never forget. Remembering your anniversary is the best way to win the heart of your partner. It will show how much you value the relationship.

5. First kiss:

If there is a single day that can hold all the essence of your relationship, it will be the day when you had your first kiss. Store this date in your memory and give a surprise to your partner by reminding them about it. Take this as one of the most effective relationship tips.

6. Appointments:

If you have promised an outing or party to your partner, there is no chance that you can escape from it later. So the only thing that you can do is to remember the date. If you remind them about the promise, nothing will make them happy than that.

7. Your first trip:

Have you ever tried to remind your partner about the good old memorable moments? Try it this time by reminding them about the day when you had your first trip together and enjoy the surprise in your partner's eye.

CHAPTER 26

Keeping Your Commitments

Commitment is a funny word. The first definition in the Encarta® World English Dictionary describes it as something that takes up time or energy - not a very appealing proposition! The third definition says it's an activity that cannot be avoided. Yikes! The fifth definition refers to the act of confinement to a mental health facility.

No wonder commitment within relationships is so tricky!

Only the second definition speaks to what we tend to mean when couples talk about commitment: devotion or dedication to a person or relationship. So, how do we wade through the other possibilities and make devotion and dedication the cornerstone of our bonds?

Let's start by looking at the negative experiences of "commitment:" we're losing energy, feeling trapped, maybe acting a little crazy. How did we get there? All too often, it's by taking things personally.

You know the drill: your wife comes home grumpy from work and somehow it feels like it's your fault. Your boyfriend is stressed about a deadline, and you find yourself walking around on tiptoe. Your lover trips over the coffee table and you apologize. After another fight with your partner, you're wondering if maybe you're just no good at this relationship thing.

We can fall prey to taking things personally in any arena, but it's especially insidious in love relationships. We know this person better than anyone in the world, right? So, of course we can tell just how much their actions or reactions are really about us.

But in reality we typically far overestimate our own impact - and in doing so, we sow the seeds of our own hesitancy to commit. By taking responsibility for their reactions, we inflate our own sense of importance and responsibility, but at the same time we create a losing proposition: why would we sign up for being permanently responsible for every peevish partner mood, every unfortunate incident, every failed communication or relationship snag?

How do we get ourselves into this way of thinking? Well, imagine a board meeting where all your worst insecurities have gathered to figure out how you should be running your life. Let's call them The Board of Mis-Directors. They'll tell you what you did wrong, where you're likely to fail, why others are laughing (or sneering) at you, how suspicious or angry you should be. And they will insist that you must take things personally.

They yank on our need to know ourselves as significant, to know that we matter to our beloved (heck, to anyone) - sending us into spasms of worry and concern. This drama creates an illusion of importance, but let's get real: do we really want to measure our significance by whether or not our spouse is grouchy today?

In reality, taking things personally distorts our perceptions, wildly inflates our worst fears, and keeps us endlessly distracted from what really matters as we try to read meaning into irrelevant details.

The truth is: what your loved one does has astonishingly little to do with you. And that's good news!

There are so many things that affect how any one of us behaves. There's our upbringing, our culture, our personality, and our past experiences. There's the time of day, the time of the month, and the influence of the stars. There's the music we're listening to, the news we just heard, or whether or not we have a headache. (And this, as you well know, is not an exhaustive list!)

When we keep this in mind, it's much easier to remember why we're in this relationship in the first place. Chances are that you've chosen intimacy because you're interested in who your partner is - what is going on for them, what motivates them, how they see and experience the world.

What if instead of taking your loved one's actions personally you paused and asked the question: "What else could be going on here?" Now you no longer have your back against the wall, wondering how you ever got yourself into this relationship and where's the nearest exit. Instead, you've asked an important question about someone you care about.

Devotion is being authentically interested in that answer. Dedication is being an honest companion, able to listen, support and challenge them in the places where their reality meets yours. Commitment gets a whole lot easier from there.

CHAPTER 27

Do Things For Each Other

Before you motivate your partner, understand the true meaning of MOTIVATION itself. The inner power or energy as you may so call it, which propels you to act and move towards your goals. Often, an individual has the desire to achieve a certain goal, but lacks the push. This is where you can step in and motivate your partner to achieve their dreams and goals and in the process strengthen your relationship. Make your partner realize the value of their ambitions. Help them assert themselves and provide them with courage, and the persistence to achieve their dreams.

To motivate your partner, know the distinction between positive & negative motivation. Positive motivation includes being optimistic in every task and negative motivation has pessimism for fear of undesirable results. Lack of motivation could hamper your partner's foresight, relations, social circle and career. There are a few things you could do to boost that much needed MOMENTUM + OPTIMISM.

Boost their confidence. It is very normal to give up easily on things that are hard to achieve. Staying on path can be a struggle at times when the goal's time-frame is for long periods. The self-doubt would nag your partner's thoughts. If you can supply positive re-enforcement regularly, you could see them to be much happier.

Appreciate the attempts:

Human beings by nature do not like being told what to do. Your partner is no different. Give them the credit for their attempts and provide subtle encouragement to achieve more. It is these attempts that will go a long way in achieving the end result.

Your contributions:

To inspire your partner, volunteer to pitch in some work towards accomplishment of their goals. Once they see your enthusiasm, it will trigger the team spirit and work wonders on your relationship.

Provide freedom:

Humans make error and learn from it. Your partner should be allowed to make mistakes to be doubly productive in their approach towards accomplishing their goals. The sense of achievement that they derive from your unconditional support will boost them up.

Motivating your partner, is also extremely beneficial for you as you can partake in the efforts, process and the accomplishments equally. You will also feel rewarded by their admiration for you. After all, when we motivate each other, we experience the joy and togetherness that life offers.

CHAPTER 28

Surprise Each Other

Surprises can always excite everyone whenever there is a special occasion or just on ordinary days. There are also many ways that you can actually surprise someone and whether it is a friend, family, or even loved ones. Surprises sometimes express the feelings of person giving it. Some surprises are better than others when it comes to your partner. How can you surprise your partner?

Here's how.

To surprise your partner, be sure that you know whether he or she likes surprises because not everyone likes them. And do not be afraid to surprise your partner and think that he or she would not like it. That is why you need to remember your partner's likes and dislikes so you can have an idea of what surprise you can come up with.

To surprise your partner, you need to make an effort so be prepared for everything and anything that could happen. Choosing the right surprise for your partner would mean choosing an activity that you both love. Or things that both of you like. Try to find what your partner likes from your conversations.

Aside from surprising your partner with things to show your love for him or her, you can actually surprise him or her with tickets. These tickets are not ordinary tickets to movies houses but rather a vacation or taking another honeymoon. This is a way to take the breath away of your partner. This will let your partner feel that you really want to spent more time together and refresh your married life.

Well, if you do not want a surprise that worth too much money, then to surprise your partner with list of activities can be a good idea. This idea would likely be activities you and your partner like to do especially when you were still boyfriend and girlfriend. This is to remember the times when you had your happy and worst times and yet you came up loving and marrying each other.

The most important thing in surprising your partner with anything is that you want to spend more time with each other. The presence of the one you love and spending your time with him or her is the most important and the most special surprise that you can give to your partner especially if you have a busy schedule all day. Time is always an issue to you and your partner when it comes to married life. So, have some time to relax with your partner.

CHAPTER 29

Encourage And Compliment

When you receive a compliment, it makes you feel great about yourself and it can really make your day, but how good are you at giving compliments to your partner? Sometimes, when you are with the same person every day, you can start to take for granted that they always look good, or that they have done well at something, but we all need a little bit of encouragement which a sincere compliment can provide. It means even more when it comes from a person we love.

Don't let your partner's efforts and achievements go unnoticed, compliment them today. Here are ten reasons why that compliment could be so important to them.

1. It will show that you notice what they do

It's a common joke that husbands don't even notice when their wife changes her hair, but men aren't the only ones that are guilty of not noticing things. When did you last compliment your man on his haircut, or the new pair of shoes he bought? Compliments are a way of showing that you are paying attention and that you do care about what your partner does.

2. It reaffirms your attraction to your partner

Compliments are a way of telling your partner that you still find him attractive, so, if he's lost few pounds lately, tell him how great his new, slim and trim figure looks. Anyone can get a bit insecure about their looks sometimes, so it never hurts to tell your partner that you still think they are hot.

3. It provides motivation

A little compliment, here and there, will inspire your partner to try even harder the next time. If he just toiled and sweated over putting a shelf up for you, tell him what a great job he's done, and he'll be more willing to get on with decorating the spare room you've been asking him to do for the past year. If he knows that you admire his handiwork, he's going to want more of those compliments, so he'll soon be onto the next job for you.

4. It will build self confidence

When you receive compliments at home, it can build your confidence in all aspects of your life. If you tell your partner how smart he looks, just before he sets off for a job interview, he's going to stride into that interview room brimming with confidence and he'll make a much better impression.

When he knows that someone he cares about thinks that he's great, other people's opinions won't matter so much to him, so he'll feel a lot stronger and more confident of his own abilities.

5. It makes the relationship a more positive one

A relationship that is filled with mutual compliments will be a far more positive relationship than one filled with constant criticism. There will always be disagreements and differences of opinion, but when they are set off by compliments, those difficult times won't seem to be as important as they might have been. Acknowledging what is good about your partner and commenting on it will create a positive feeling about the relationship.

6. Compliments can be good for both of you

Giving your partner compliments can be good for you too, because it reminds you of the things that you love about them.

We are all usually very quick to point out the faults in our partners and give them a hard time when they do something wrong. Balancing that with few compliments will help you to see what's right about the relationship too.

7. You'll get more compliments in return

All this complimenting won't be a one way thing. Once you start the ball rolling, you'll find that your partner wakes up the power of compliments too. You don't want it become some kind of mutual appreciation society, that would be so false, but a little bit if two-way appreciation is never a bad thing in a relationship.

8. It will make your partner more creative

A compliment might even help your husband think his way through a problem he's been stuck on. He could have a problem at work that you don't know about and you telling him how impressed you are by the way he usually handles things could be just what he needs to inspire him to solve that problem. It's strange, but when people are told they are good something, they usually become even better at it.

9. It will cultivate an atmosphere of appreciation and gratitude

As much as anything, a compliment shows your appreciation for your partner and that will stop him from feeling like he is being taken for granted. Being noticed and being appreciated are things that we all need, because it tells us when we are getting things right.

10. It's an easy way to make your partner feel good.

CHAPTER 30

Role Of Personal Growth

Growth is the essence of life. We are meant to keep growing throughout our lives yet so many people settle for stagnating, repetitive lives. I am talking about emotional growing: taking responsibility to take good care of body, mind, and spirit. The end result is, and studies verify it, that too many people are feeling bored, lonely, unchallenged, and depressed.

How Personal Growth Improves Relationships?

1. Improved Attitude

When you are taking good care of yourself you have a better attitude about life. You feel energized and enjoy the process of growing yourself. You have a clearer sense of what matters to you and you see other people objectively.

2. Personal change influences relationships

When you feel more energized, you want your relationship to have more energy also. You accept that your changes will affect the relationship and you work positively at enhancing the relationship.

3. Introduce changes that enhance self and the relationship

As you engage in personal growth it becomes important to you that your relationships also grow. You introduce changes being respectful of the other person and expect that initially there will be resistance. Ultimately, as positive self-growth change is introduced relationships can become stronger.

How to Increase Personal Growth?

1. Embrace Change

Most of what we do is automatic. We unconsciously go through the days, repeating what we have done the day before. Value that you want to keep growing. Decide on one habit that you would like to change. Make it small enough so you can easily remember it and have success when you do it. In time, you will add other things that will lead to personal growth.

2. Create Energy

In order to enjoy life you have to have energy. Energy is physical and mental. We get energy by exercising regularly, eating energy producing foods, and stimulating our minds. Start establishing rituals for creating energy for yourself.

3. Engage in Life

Engage with life. One of the fundamental truisms is that to be engaged in life you have to be present in the present. Not just going through the repetitive motions but really engaging in the here and now. Seeing things around you, listening to what is being said, engaging in life with all your senses.

CONCLUSION

Every relationship has its different stages, and although one hopes endlessly for a secret formula to make a relationship work, the secret actually lies within us. It completely depends on our ability to deal with things and make things work for the better. The excitement about falling in love is universal, but to maintain the relationship takes more effort than you could ever think of!

Although there are predictable stages of being in love, a healthy relationship is far more different from just being in love. If you are often confused where your relationship is headed to or if you often wish to have and maintain a healthy relationship, take a look at some of the stages of a healthy relationship given below. These stages might help you to understand and overcome any shortcomings in your current relationship.

Stages of Relationships

Wooing Your Love

This stage is most popular and common with many of us. The feeling of falling in love and the sleepless nights that follows are an obvious indication you wish to spend more time with each other. This is the time a couple uses to create a better impression on each other. Roses, scented candles, chocolates, and teddy bears ... gift shops perhaps would never have seen their cash registers ringing if it weren't for couples madly in love! Wooing one's love in great style is the obvious beginning to a relationship, and the joy of acceptance from a partner is something that cannot be described!

Emotional Attachment

A healthy relationship is possible only when you feel a mutual attachment for each other. Emotional attachment is the mainstay of any relationship for that matter; this forms a foundation to build a future together! This is the time when you can probably call him/her at odd hours.

He/she would be the first person you ring up to convey your happiness or share a sorrowful moment. This is one of the most important stages of a healthy relationship as it is during this phase when you begin to unbosom yourselves and trust each other as well.

Physical Intimacy

Let's face it; a certain level of physical intimacy is required for a healthy relationship. Physical attraction towards your partner is important and natural as long as you do not get obsessed with the same. This is the period when you wish to spend every waking hour with him/her, but learning to curb those feelings to a certain extent would help form a firm base for a healthy relationship.

Physical attraction when based on your emotional feelings rather than just outward appearance would help you to have a meaningful relationship rather than just a fling. Emotional intimacy is the foremost thing if you are looking for stability in relationships. Although it's not a crime being physically attracted to your partner, you should know where to draw the line.

Strengthening the Bond of Friendship

Having your partner as your best friend is one of the best stages of a healthy relationship. Being friends with each other will help to bring you closer with your partner and also increase the trust element between each other. Considering your partner as a friend is also a sign of acceptance.

It means you have accepted him/her completely and share a certain level of maturity between each other. Every meaningful relationship of our life germinates from friendship, and so if you have it with your partner, you have unlocked the door to having a healthy relationship.

Dealing with Flaws

After all the initial euphoria of being in love, comes the stage of discovering each other's flaws! Learning to deal with your partner's shortcomings is an important stage in any healthy relationship. At times, certain traits of a person are probably visible only as time flies by. Short tempers and attitude problems are some things you may have to deal with once you are in the relationship.

Recognizing your partner's problem area is another important stage required to maintain a healthy relationship. Learning to deal with it and sorting the issues amicably will only strengthen your relation with each other.

Retaining Individual Identities

No matter how much amount of compromise is involved in a relationship, you must retain your individuality to some extent. Being a doormat has not helped any couple; in fact, it only tends to worsen things for the couple. Know yourself from within and mold yourself only for the better.

At this stage, when you both maintain your individuality and respect each other for what you are, it would be a step towards the right direction for any relationship.

Commitment Levels Between the Couple

Falling in love is easy, but being in love for a long period of time requires commitment. Commitment towards each other is required for any relationship if you wish to have one that's for keeps! A commitment towards each other only helps to establish more faith you have for each other. This means that both of you will have to be transparent and unambiguous about each other's lives.

Likewise, both partners need to be ready for commitment to have a healthy relationship. The stage of commitment is reached when couples realize they have common goals and would want to spend every bit of their joys and sorrows with each other. Marriage is something you can decide later, and if you both are willing to take the plunge, then having complete faith in each other is requisite.

These stages of a healthy relationship should help you to analyze your relationship and know where it's headed. With a little bit of understanding, love, and care, you would have the right recipe for a successful relationship!

Attributes of a Healthy Relationship

To know whether you are in the right relationship or not, you need to be first of all aware of the traits of a healthy relationship.

Communication and Friendship

I read somewhere that a person should always marry someone they love to talk to and are good friends with. As years pass on, the initial physical attraction tends to fail. At this point, only if the partners are good friends and love to communicate with one another, can they keep the spark alive in their relationship. So, one of the most important signs of a good relationship is a strong friendship bond and open communication.

Respect and Trust

Respecting one another's opinions, ways of living, careers, etc. is very essential. If you find your partner constantly criticizing you or is unnecessarily overbearing, it means that he or she does not respect or appreciate you enough. Besides respect, trust between both the partners is very important too. Commitment and honesty are the two pillars on which a relationship stands.

Love and Intimacy

Deep love for one another and a feeling of belonging is a must in a relationship. If you and your partner see this relationship as something long term, if you both are good and comfortable at expressing love for one another by way of kisses and hugs, if you share the right sexual chemistry and meet each other's physical needs - all these are traits of a good relationship.

Willingness to Give, Change and Support

This is very important. Both the partners should be willing to give alot of love and support to one another. They should be willing to change, compromise and adjust a bit to meet their partner's needs. Admitting to and correcting one's mistakes, listening patiently to what the other has to say and by being open-minded, any couple can form a healthy relationship.

Life Beyond One Another

Partners in a healthy relationship have a life of their own. They have their own set of friends, interests, works, etc. away from their partner. In a relationship, time with one's partner, "me time" i.e. time alone with oneself as well as time away from one's partner, pursuing things that one likes to do - all are equally important. So if you see yourself as well as your partner, as independent yet loving individuals, you are in a healthy relationship.

Skillful Communication Tips That Promise You a Happy Relationship

Communication is a very crucial part of our lives, especially when it comes to relationships. In order for a relationship to run smoothly, there should be effective communication between both partners. By improving communication skills, you will be able to understand the feelings of the other person clearly and effectively. Understanding the importance will even help you prevent and overcome any misunderstanding between both partners.

Listen Carefully

There are many things that we mess up just because we miss out on listening to what the other person actually wants to say. This can even happen in a relationship. When communicating with your partner, don't just hear but listen carefully.

This will enable you to understand what the other person is saying and prepare for a response. While listening, do not interrupt the other person. If you do so, it would naturally show your disinterest in the matter.

Speak Clearly

Just like careful listening, speaking clearly is also a very significant point when it comes to good communication skills. What you speak has to be balanced with what you have heard. Do not overstate what you want to say and be clear. While speaking, it is always better to consider the other person's point of view. Do not be rude or one-sided in your talk with your partner, and most importantly, do not criticize.

Understand Body Language

Body language is another essential aspect of good communication in relationships. If you want to reach greater depths in understanding each other, you also need to use body language in your communication. Along with just plain listening and speaking, you also have to include body language as a part of your communication. This includes eye movements, posture, and other facial expressions. Good body language can be used in order to show interest in the communication.

Use the 'I' Word Correctly

The 'I' word plays a very important role when it comes to clear communication in relationships. Using 'I' in your statements gives an impression that what is being said is your point of view, and the views can differ. Instead of using the statement 'You make me frustrated', it is a good option to say 'I don't like it when this happens'. This makes the conversation less accusatory and makes the other person feel that he is not being totally blamed.

Other Skills

You should communicate in a way that would create a kind of mutual understanding between both partners. The communication should essentially lead to a solution and not more complications in the conflict. In some cases, physical touch can even contribute to good understanding in both partners. For instance, just holding hands while talking can be of great help to pass on the message effectively.

Let go of the ego

It is also important to accept that you are wrong if you really are. Learn to appreciate your partner to enhance the quality of your communication. Another good idea is to turn a complaint into a request by saying please and other such words. Instead of shouting 'You never say goodbye!', you can just say 'Can you please say goodbye while going?'.

These are some of the most effective skills in relationships that you need to develop. There are many other skills that you would develop over time after following these tips. Remember that being a good communicator with your partner will make the bond stronger and long lasting.

About The Author

Vishal Pandey, author & publisher, was born in Lucknow, India. After completing post graduation in management, he joined the corporate world, only to realize quickly that it was not the path for him. His decade-old passion for self-development led him to the world of writing and creation of his blog.

Over the course of fourteen years, he read hundreds of books, listened to audio/video programs, attended seminars on the topic of personal development and tested every piece of information by applying it in real life.

His blog was originally created to share this information with the world but later evolved into a platform for mutual interaction with his readers. After receiving several requests to write a book from his readers, he wrote 'Positive Thinking', followed by 'Happiness Edge' and more.

Besides writing, he loves meditation, yoga, martial arts, music, nutrition, psychology, and travelling.

You can contact him at:

Email: yourselfactualization@gmail.com

Facebook: facebook.com/selfactualization.co

Twitter: @selfactualized9

MORE BOOKS BY VISHAL PANDEY

Positive Thinking: What It Really Takes To Free Yourself from Negativity

The Happiness Edge: The Eight Principles of Happiness to Gain Competitive Advantage in Business and Life

Happiness for Beginners

Social Success: Be Likeable, Create Instant Rapport and Influence People

The Magic of Positive Thinking

Gratitude: Getting In Touch With What Really Matters

Forgiveness: The Greatest Cure for a Suffering Heart

Happiness Within: A revolutionary understanding of happiness and fulfillment

Success Habits of High Achievers

Books by Vishal Pandey:

Positive Thinking: How to Stop Focusing on Nonsense and Live a Better Life

The sole purpose of this book 'Positive Thinking' is to help readers shift to a more optimistic, positive thinking mindset in order to attain happiness and fulfillment in life.

The Search for an Answer...

The author struggled with habitual negative thoughts & low self esteem for thirteen years. His tussle with negativity drove him to the world of human psychology and behavioral science. But something was missing. Happiness and positivity still eluded him. It was not the complete solution.

His search for an answer led him to eastern philosophy. Thousands of years old wisdom perfectly complemented modern day science. Combining the two, he was able to change himself from gloomy & pessimistic to an optimistic person.

This book 'Positive Thinking' contains the most important thoughts and concepts that helped him shift his own mindset. Several myths about negative and positive thinking are debunked, guiding the reader through what really works by taking a realistic and practical approach.

End negativity and bring change at the deepest level.

Because negativity is a product of multiple issues functioning under the surface, the subject of negative and positive thinking has been broken into multiple levels. Readers are taken on a journey through "building self belief" to "improving their health & mindset" to "finding happiness within ourselves".

What you will learn inside Positive Thinking?

- How to stop taking things personally?

- How to stop depending on situations & people for happiness?

- How to change the way you see the world?

- How to belief in yourself & raise your self esteem?

- How to guard your mind from negative influences?

- How to live worry free and enjoy the present moment?

- How to diminish your worst fears?

- How to create happiness and fulfillment in your relationships?

If you aim to move towards positive thinking, happiness and high self esteem... do yourself a favor and read this book.

More Books by Vishal Pandey:

Success Habits of High Achievers

Success Habits of High Achievers is not only filled with personal stories of Icons, legends, and leaders of our generation but also contains silent victories of regular, everyday people. The high-performance habits, routines, mindset & insights highlighted by *Success Habits of High Achievers* apply to every facet of life, inspiring readers to leverage these ideas to achieve their own aspirations.

The author spent more than a decade studying the lives of the most successful people of our time. This book is about the habits, routines, thought processes and skills which allow seemingly ordinary people to accomplish extraordinary feats.

Success Habits of High Achievers will reshape the way you think about success and growth, and give you the tools and strategies you need to transform your life.

Key ideas:

- Discover the secret used by renowned leaders to gain incredible inner drive.
- Proven tips for beating procrastination.
- How to believe in yourself in the face of self-doubt?
- Strategies used by successful people to overcome failure.
- How to create a winner's mindset?
- Little things successful people do differently that makes a huge difference.
- Brain hacks to improve your focus and productivity.

- What to do when you feel overwhelmed & stressed out?
- Actionable advice & exercises throughout the book to readers who are ready to start now.

Here are the ultimate benefits you will get:

- You'll become highly productive.
- You'll be persistent in the face of challenges.
- You'll have a winner's mindset.
- You'll be highly motivated.
- You'll have a success-driven mentality.
- You'll experience success and abundance in all areas of life.

More Books by Vishal Pandey:

Social Success: Be Likeable, Create Instant Rapport and Influence People

You never get a second chance to create a great first impression.

Body language and voice tone makes up 93% of how other people perceive us.

Words only accounts for 7%.

Our first impression is made LONG BEFORE we say anything. Usually within the first 2 seconds after other people see us. If we mess it up, then it's very difficult to change people's perception of us. We NEED to master this part of our communication.

Do you want to create great first impression and build rapport with ANYONE you meet?

When trying to achieve success in ANY endeavor, it always involves interaction with other people – partners, team mates, customers, prospects, coaches, mentors, peers, family and friends. I believe that a BIG part of achieving success is improving social skills we NEED everyday.

In this book, Social Success: be likeable, create instant rapport and influence people, you will find specific behaviors and body language tips that will turn you into a social powerhouse. You'll become instantly likable and command power and influence in your social interactions.

Some of the social skills you'll learn:

* Real-world applicable techniques that'll make your communication extremely potent.

* Why we put more attention to (and trust) body language of an individual more than his words?

* How to make an interaction free-flowing as it should be?

* A simple technique to make people feel relaxed on first meeting.

* Exact step-by-step process to create a memorable impression on anyone you meet.

* How to add more fun & positivity in your interactions?

* Powerful exercises to develop a confident yet relaxed eye contact.

* How to capture and hold the attention of the entire group for as long as you want?

You'll also learn:

* 8 behaviors that are sabotaging your social skills and specific ways to avoid them, once and for all.

* Learn a secret that best communicators use to gain instant acceptance in any setting and become 'one with the crowd'.

* Learn how to deal with social pressure and two powerful exercises to strengthen your emotional resolve.

* How to eliminate friction from your relationships?

* An easy way to make anyone you meet feel special. This single people skill would boost your likability & social life to unprecedented levels.

* The critical component in gaining trust of people. People, who miss this crucial social skill, keep wondering why they are unable to persuade others.

* Learn charisma secrets of celebrities which you can use to make people addicted to you.

* The BIGGEST indicator of low confidence that may be hampering your social success. If you don't avoid it, people won't take you seriously.

…and there are more such valuable social skills and communication techniques inside the book. If you wish to master your interactions with people, read this book.

More Books by Vishal Pandey:

Gratitude: Getting in touch with what really matters

There's a saying, "*when we get old, we'll look back at our life and smile.*"

Why wait? We can start right now.

Practice of gratitude proposes daily reflection on overlooked aspects of our lives which we should be grateful for. In this fast-paced world, it's easy to lose touch with what really matters in life, things we are already blessed with.

The endless chase for happiness spans over the entire course of our life, only to realize in the end, we always had what we were searching for. The joy, peace and content we desperately wanted, was inside our hearts from the very beginning.

Nothing external can provide true, lasting happiness.

It's sad that such a profound realization normally occurs at later stages of life. We always have a choice. At any moment, we can choose to be happy and grateful. It changes our perspective. We begin to see situations in a different light.

Gratitude provides comfort in difficult times and supports us in changing the course of our lives. It's a progressive journey towards lasting inner peace and joy.

Filled with warmth, compassion and depth, 'Gratitude' empowers its readers to see things from a different, upbeat perspective and live life to the fullest.

Some of the topics covered in Gratitude:

- How gratitude increase happiness in ways money can't?

- How gratitude makes you more empathic and improves all your relationships?

- Why forgiveness is an important part of being grateful?

- The step-by-step explanation of gratitude practice.

- The world is both good & bad. We decide what we focus on.

- How we can change the meaning of anything which happens in life?

- Finding overlooked aspects of our life that we should be grateful for.

More Books by Vishal Pandey:

The Magic of Positive Thinking

Do you constantly repeat a negative thought over and over for hours? A past event makes you feel horrible for long periods of time? Do you worry excessively over something? Do you feel extremely nervous & anxious about an upcoming situation?

In this follow-up sequel to the bestseller "Positive Thinking: what it really takes to free yourself from negativity", author shares his very best ideas and practical exercises which helped him overcome a decade long depression and negative thinking habit.

'The Magic of Positive Thinking' will allow readers to see positivity from multiple angles - science, philosophy and spirituality - and lead them to a place of deeper understanding of how our thoughts and emotions work.

This book builds upon its predecessor, but it's not mandatory for readers to read the previous book.

A glance at the topics covered:

- How to stop repeating negative thoughts over & over in your mind?

- Break the habit of constantly worrying.

- How to build confidence and certainty for future instead of fear/anxiety?

- Learn to see people & situations from a different, uplifting perspective.

- How an empowering morning routine changes your whole day for the better?

- How to forgive people and be grateful for what you have in life?

- Why sometimes experiencing pain is fine and even necessary for a better future?

- How to let go of negative experiences of the past and feel content in the present?

- How to break bad habits and replace them with positive ones?

- End chaos and bring order in your everyday life.

You deserve to be happy. You deserve to live a happy, positive life. It all really begins with your thoughts. Break the chain of continuous negative thoughts and move towards a life filled with love and joy. Use the insights and exercises in the book to transform your day.

Do not delay. Start your journey to a place of positivity and happiness.

More Books by Vishal Pandey:

The Happiness Edge

Do you rely on money, people and material things for your happiness?

I'll never work. Period.

Anything outside of you could never provide long term happiness and peace. We have been brainwashed by society to think if we get THAT... we would be so happy. If that were the case, why a lot of people who seemingly have all the money, fame and admiration feel depressed and resort to drugs for happiness?

Happiness is always created from within and it always flows from inside-out.

In this insightful book, readers will learn how to shift their focus from external temptations to things which really fills our life with happiness so we could share it with others.

"*Happiness is not what you get... happiness is what you do & become.*"

It is time to end the eternal chase for more and put life in perspective that is empowering and uplifting.

- How to feel content with what we have?

- How focusing on little positive things which happen every day will change your life?

- What is emotional energy and how it changes your entire day?

- How to find something positive in almost every situation and transform your world?

- Impact of your body on the amount of happiness you experience.

- Daily exercises to release stress from your body & mind completely.

- How to become more resilient to negative thoughts?

- How our social interactions shape our life?

We have been blindly following what society told us till now. It's time to debunk what we learned from social conditioning and face the truth about happiness.

Filled with practical insights and exercises, 'Happiness' would help its readers achieve sense of peace and joy that has eluded us so far. We have one life. We get one chance. Make it the best it could possibly be.

Do not wait anymore. Get the book and prepare for a complete transformation.

More Books by Vishal Pandey:

Forgiveness: The Greatest Cure for a Suffering Heart

Something has happened in your life that is causing a lot of inner pain. While it's perfectly normal to feel bad about an unpleasant experience, we may end up holding on to these negative feelings for a time longer than necessary.

The longer we hold on to bitter feelings, the more influence they get over our lives. We start to habitually judging people & situation based on our past.

Don't let stories of the past control our present & future...

At any moment, we have a choice. We can either hold on to anger or we could let it go. Forgiveness is a healing process that liberates you from the wounds of the past.

Forgiveness doesn't mean we forget what happened in the past. It's more about releasing our negative emotions we have associated with a past experience.

In 'Forgiveness', readers are introduced to a step-by-step process of releasing negative emotions and making peace with people, places, situations and ultimately, their past.

The book proposes the idea of looking deep within ourselves and rooting out negative emotions from our core. Stop self-blame, judgment, fear and victim mentality and live life of peace, content & joy.

CPSIA information can be obtained
at www.ICGtesting.com
Printed in the USA
LVHW090137291019
635549LV00006B/2012/P